Original title:

Elder Looms Over the Phoenix Jug

Author: Liina Liblikas

ISBN HARDBACK: 978-1-80563-195-8

ISBN PAPERBACK: 978-1-80564-716-4

Keeper of the Solar Embrace

In the realm where shadows dance,
Beneath the moonlit glimmer,
A keeper waits with outstretched hands,
Holding light as days grow dimmer.

With every sunset's fiery glow,
He whispers secrets to the stars,
Planting dreams where dark winds blow,
Mending hearts with solar scars.

On golden wings of twilight's grace,
He casts his warmth across the land,
Guiding souls in endless chase,
To find their dreams as grains of sand.

Through fields where wishes softly weave,
He dances with the fading light,
A gentle lull, the world to leave,
As night encroaches, bold and bright.

Yet in his heart, a flicker stays,
The promise of the dawn anew,
For after darkness, sunlight plays,
And hope will ever guide us through.

Rebirth in the Keeper's Eyes

In twilight's grasp, whispers dwell,
A keeper's heart, an ancient spell.
Through shadows deep, a flicker calls,
As destiny weaves through silent halls.

A glimmer sparks in emerald light,
A soul reborn takes ancient flight.
With every breath, the past ignites,
Awakening dreams in starry nights.

Echoes of laughter, pain, and love,
Binding spirits like clouds above.
In keeper's eyes, the truth resides,
Where hope and sorrow gently bides.

Flames of Memory and Renewal

In flickering embers, stories burn,
Lessons whispered, waiting turn.
Forgotten flames of yesterdays,
Their warmth ignites, in many ways.

A dance of shadows on the wall,
Tales of glory, rise and fall.
With ashes strewn beneath the sky,
The heart remembers, the soul will fly.

New flames arise from scattered fates,
Forging bonds that time creates.
Through fire's lens, the truth is known,
In every heart, the seeds are sown.

The Fire's Aged Prophecy

In the ember's glow, secrets spin,
Whispers of fate beneath the skin.
Ancient texts on pages worn,
Foretelling dreams where hope is born.

A dance of sparks, a phoenix hue,
Casting shadows for me and you.
In the quiet, a prophecy waits,
Illuminating unseen gates.

Beneath the stars, so vast and bright,
Burns a fire that brings the night.
With every flicker, futures show,
Through fire's lens, the ages flow.

The Sentinel's Glowing Reverie

Amidst the stone, the sentinel lies,
A guardian lost in reverie skies.
With memories woven in the breeze,
He watches over, hearts at ease.

Glimmers of laughter fill the air,
Echoes of love, forever rare.
In his gaze, the world unfolds,
A tapestry of stories told.

The sentinel stands, steadfast and bright,
Illuminating the darkest night.
In glowing dreams, he finds his place,
A ward for those who seek solace.

The Resilient Watcher's Gaze

In twilight's veil, a figure stands,
With eyes that spark like ancient sands.
Each whisper soft, like secrets told,
A guardian's heart, steadfast and bold.

Through storms that howl and skies that weep,
The watcher stirs, though shadows creep.
Their gaze holds strength, a quiet might,
Against the dark, they forge the light.

Time may bend, yet they remain,
A sentinel through joy and pain.
They hold the past, the present near,
With every glance, they quell the fear.

In hidden realms, where spirits roam,
The watcher stays, forever home.
With wisdom deep as ocean's breath,
They challenge fate and dance with death.

A flicker bright in endless night,
Their presence warms, a guiding light.
Through trials faced and sorrows borne,
The resilient watcher greets the dawn.

Guardianship of the Resurgent Ember

From ashes cold, a glow ascends,
A spark of hope that never bends.
In hidden depths, where shadows hide,
The ember waits, its strength and pride.

With gentle breath, the flames restore,
A dance of light on whispered lore.
The guardians stand with hearts ablaze,
To fan the fire, the hopeful gaze.

Each flicker tells of battles fought,
Of lessons learned, of battles sought.
They guard the warmth with tender grace,
And nurture dreams in sacred space.

Around the hearth, the stories weave,
Of courage found and hearts that cleave.
The ember's glow ignites the night,
With flickering tales of boundless light.

When darkness falls and shadows creep,
The ember's warmth is ours to keep.
With every spark, a promise breathes,
The guardians' vow, our hope achieves.

In the Shadow of the Eternal Blaze

Beneath the glow of ceaseless flame,
A world awaits, forever the same.
In shadows cast, the whispers dwell,
Of stories long, no tongue could tell.

The blaze consumes, yet none it breaks,
In warmth embraced, the silence wakes.
Within the flicker, strength resides,
As time flows like the restless tides.

Among the ashes, lifetimes weave,
In every heart, a space to grieve.
Yet hope ignites, where darkness lies,
In fragments lost, the spirit flies.

The shimmer dances, a fleeting shade,
In every heart, a promise made.
In the blaze's heart, we find our place,
In shadows deep, we hold our grace.

For every fire that fades away,
Beneath the stars, we learn to play.
In the embrace of flames that rise,
We stand together, 'neath endless skies.

The Phoenix's Silent Keeper

In moonlit nights, a figure lies,
The guardian of the phoenix cries.
With gentle hands, they cradle flame,
A keeper silent, without name.

Through cycles wrought with fire and ash,
The keeper holds, their heart a stash.
Memories blend like dusk and dawn,
In whispered hopes, the phoenix spawns.

With wings unfurled, the bird takes flight,
While shadows dance, a wondrous sight.
The keeper smiles, a tear set free,
For every life, a legacy.

In every rise, there's beauty found,
Among the ashes, glory crowned.
The silent keeper knows this tale,
Of love and loss, in every scale.

With every birth, a flame renewed,
In sacred trust, their hearts imbued.
The phoenix soars, the keeper waits,
For hope in flight, as life creates.

Prophecies Engulfed in Flame

In the dusk where shadows weave,
Whispers of fate begin to cleave.
Ancient texts in candle's glow,
Tell of trials no heart should know.

A fire burns with secrets old,
In flickering tongues, tales are told.
With each ember a wish takes flight,
Hope ignites in the heart of night.

Lost in ashes, truth will bloom,
Rising forth from grief and gloom.
Fate entwined with sparks and light,
Guides the brave through endless night.

In the blaze, a vision glows,
Of realms where the soft wind blows.
Chasing dreams that fate has spun,
From the ashes, a new day's begun.

So heed the flames, for in their dance,
Lies the power of fate's chance.
In the embers, the past will call,
Through infernos, we rise or fall.

Flight of Timeless Spirits

Beneath the stars, the spirits soar,
Dancing through the endless lore.
Their whispers tickle the midnight air,
A symphony beyond compare.

On wings of longing, they glide free,
Travelers through eternity.
Carrying tales of joy and strife,
They weave the fabric of our life.

With every flutter, worlds collide,
Past and future walk beside.
In the silence, wisdom reigns,
And the heart remembers pains.

Longing glimmers in their flight,
Guiding hearts toward the light.
From shadows deep, they lead us on,
To discover where we belong.

So when the night is dark and wide,
And dreams are swept with the tide,
Remember spirits guide your quest,
In their embrace, find your rest.

The Ancient Heart of the Phoenix

In the cradle of embers bright,
Beats the heart of the endless night.
A creature forged in flames and tears,
Whispers legends throughout the years.

With feathers like the setting sun,
It rises high when all seems done.
From ashes cold, it takes its flight,
A symbol of the fight for light.

In every burn, a story grows,
Of battles lost, and triumphs glows.
It sings of rebirth with every flare,
In its presence, no soul will despair.

For in the fire, power sings,
A melody of wondrous things.
The ancient heart, forever bold,
Holds the truths that were once told.

So let the phoenix rise anew,
In every heart, its flame is true.
In darkness find that vibrant spark,
And carry hope through the night's stark.

Ashes Adorned with Wisdom's Light

Where silence falls on sacred ground,
In ashes deep, the truth is found.
Fables whisper through the dust,
In every grain, abide the trust.

Wisdom shines like silver stars,
Guiding souls through hidden wars.
Each ember tells of paths once trod,
Where heartache meets the hand of God.

From ashes rise the dreams once lost,
Though trials come, we bear the cost.
A tapestry of hope unfurls,
In the quiet, a new world swirls.

Embrace the lessons time imparts,
For in the dark, the soul ignites.
Adorned in light, the wise emerge,
With every step, the past converges.

So tread with care, and learn from pain,
In wisdom's glow, we break the chain.
Through ashes' veil, the light shall gleam,
In every heart, a living dream.

Echoes of the Ashen Protector

In shadows deep, where whispers play,
A guardian stands, come what may.
With heart of ember, fierce and bright,
He watches over, through the night.

The winds do weave a tale untold,
Of battles won, of legends bold.
With each soft rustle, echoes sigh,
Of ancient spirits, soaring high.

The ashes dance, in moonlit beams,
Reviving long-forgotten dreams.
Through tangled woods where secrets lie,
The protector's watch shall never die.

In every heart, the embers glow,
The strength to rise, the will to grow.
In timeless realms, where magics blend,
Echoes of courage shall not end.

The Seer Beneath Ashen Skies

Beneath the veil of muted gray,
A seer waits for night and day.
With eyes that pierce the shadows' veil,
She sees the threads that twist and sail.

Her whispered words, a gentle breeze,
Reveal the fates, the dark to seize.
In patterns wrought of twinkling stars,
She glimpses all, from near to far.

With fingertips that trace the air,
She conjures visions, hope and care.
A tapestry of life unfolds,
As stories woven, softly told.

In dreams she walks, in silence speaks,
With wisdom deep, for truth she seeks.
Beneath the ash, beneath the sky,
The seer's gift shall never die.

Gilded Visions from the Past

In twilight's glow, the shadows fade,
Where history's threads and futures wade.
Gilded visions, lost in time,
A symphony of tales that rhyme.

The echoes of laughter, soft and sweet,
In distant halls, where memories meet.
With whispers that ripple through the air,
Fragments of yore, beyond compare.

Each golden glimmer, a story spun,
From battles fought, to love begun.
In every corner, secrets rise,
Gilded visions beneath the skies.

The past entwined with present's grace,
A dance eternal, time can't erase.
In every heartbeat, shadows blend,
Gilded visions that transcend.

Flames of Wisdom in the Twilight

As daylight wanes and shadows creep,
The flames of wisdom stir from sleep.
With colors bright, they flicker bold,
A beacon warm, a light to hold.

In quiet murmurs, secrets flow,
The ancient truths begin to show.
Each crackle speaks of paths once trod,
Of lessons learned, beneath the odd.

With fire's grace, they dance and sway,
Illuminating the shadows play.
In twilight's grasp, their tales ignite,
Flames of wisdom, shining bright.

They beckon forth the lost and weary,
With stories rich, yet oft so dreary.
In every flame, a life unfurls,
Wisdom's warmth within life's whirl.

The Keeper Behind the Flame

In the heart of the twilight glow,
A keeper whispers secrets low.
With flickering light, shadows twist,
In the dance of fire, none can resist.

Through the ages, embers gleam,
Guarding dreams that softly beam.
A flicker here, a spark of fate,
In the stillness, they quietly await.

Bound by duty, the flames do sigh,
Revealing truths that never die.
With every crackle, stories unfold,
Of bravery, warmth, and courage bold.

Ink-stained pages in a swirling breeze,
Memories linger with utmost ease.
The keeper watches, ever so wise,
In the glow, where destinies rise.

So heed the flame, its gentle song,
For it binds the lost and the strong.
A keeper's heart, forever it stands,
Guiding souls with glowing hands.

The Sorcerer of Smoldering Hearts

In shadows deep, a sorcerer waits,
With smoldering hearts that fan the fates.
His gaze ignites the quiet chills,
As magic swirls, and courage fills.

With whispered spells and ancient lore,
He stirs the embers, ignites the core.
In the silence, a promise unfurls,
A dance of flames, in fantasy swirls.

His heart is fierce like the raging fire,
Fueling dreams, igniting desire.
From ashes, hope and passion rise,
In the warmth of love, a bond never dies.

Through twilight paths, he weaves his thread,
Connecting worlds where wonders spread.
Each flicker tells a tale untold,
Of smoldering hearts, and spirits bold.

So if you seek the sorcerer's grace,
Embrace the glow, find your place.
For in the warmth of a kindled spark,
Awaits a journey, bright in the dark.

Gaze of the Eternal Guardian

In the night sky, a guardian gleams,
With vigilant eyes, weaving dreams.
A watchful gaze on realms below,
In the quiet, the secrets flow.

Under the stars, he guards the flame,
Protecting hope, forever the same.
With a heart of courage, pure and bright,
He shields the world from endless night.

Through storms of doubt and whispers of fear,
His eternal presence draws us near.
In the flicker of light, we find our way,
Guided by love, come what may.

With every flicker, the guardian sings,
Of timeless wonders and hidden things.
In the ebb and flow of time's embrace,
He holds the memories, a sacred space.

So look to the stars, let your heart soar,
For the guardian's light shall evermore.
With steadfast promise, he'll light your quest,
In the gaze of the eternal, find your rest.

Flames Forged in Time's Fire

In the furnace of fate, embers blaze,
Where time forges paths in mysterious ways.
Each spark a moment, a choice, a sign,
In the dance of the flames, destinies align.

With whispers of ages, the fire speaks,
Of triumphs hard-earned and joyous peaks.
It tells of journeys through dark and light,
Of heroes rising to claim their right.

Forged in passion and tempered by dreams,
The flames flicker soft, or roar in streams.
From ashes, new beginnings take flight,
In the heart of darkness shines the light.

So gather around as the stories unfold,
In the warmth of the fire, let brave tales be told.
For the flames of time burn bright and strong,
In the hearth of history, we all belong.

With each flicker, let your spirit soar,
For in time's fire, we forevermore.
Each moment a flame, flickering free,
In the tapestry of life, our legacy.

Guardians of the Fiery Vessel

In shadows flicker whispers faint,
The guardians stand, a solemn grace,
With eyes aglow, a timeless paint,
They guard the flame, their steadfast place.

Around the hearth, the secrets weave,
Of stories sung in ember's glow,
Through trials faced, they dare believe,
A bond of fire, a heart's warm show.

Each spark a promise, bright and bold,
A legacy of strength untold,
As night descends with tales to find,
Their spirits rise, forever bind.

In every flicker, courage flies,
A beacon in the darkened night,
They hear the echoes, ancient cries,
The fiery vessel holds their light.

So gather 'round, the flames invite,
Where guardians reign, and hopes ignite.

In the Presence of the Timeless Flame

With every breath, the flame persists,
A spark of life, a dance of dreams,
In twilight's hush, the magic twists,
Around the hearth, a warmth that gleams.

Here lies the truth in flickering glow,
By ancient hands the fire is fed,
In whispered lore, the secrets flow,
Beneath the arch where dreams are bred.

Each ember speaks of love and loss,
In every crackle, wisdom dwells,
It shows the way, despite the cost,
A timeless flame, where heart compels.

With every heartbeat, shadows leap,
They dance upon the stone and wood,
Awakening promises we keep,
In the presence where hope once stood.

As night unfolds its quiet shroud,
The flame remains, a guardian proud.

Echoes of the Phoenix's Guardian

From ashes rise, the phoenix sings,
A symphony of light and fire,
With every note, the heavens ring,
A guardian's oath, a heart's desire.

Through trials fierce, the flame is found,
It flickers wild, yet stands so true,
In echoes soft, its song profound,
A promise born in vibrant hue.

In the whispers of the flames in flight,
There lies a tale of strength regained,
Each flicker holds the endless night,
In every heart, the hope remained.

Together forging timeless bonds,
Fires of courage burn bright and bold,
As phoenix rises, life responds,
Guardian's tale of truths retold.

So let the fire blaze anew,
A dance of strength that shall not dim.

Beneath the Gaze of Wisdom

In quietude, the wise ones stand,
With timeless eyes that pierce the veil,
They watch the world, a steady hand,
In silent grace, their tales unveil.

The flickering flame reflects their thought,
Each ember holds a world within,
In wisps of smoke, the lessons taught,
A guardian's smile beneath the din.

Through trials faced, they weave their lore,
A tapestry of light and shade,
In every heartbeat, wisdom's core,
The guidance found in joys portrayed.

With reverent hearts and open minds,
They offer solace, strength, and peace,
In guardianship, the true heart binds,
Where wisdom blooms, and fears release.

So gather close and heed the flame,
Beneath its gaze, the heart's true aim.

Ashes Cradle Phoenix Dreams

In twilight whispers, dreams ignite,
From ashes rising, taking flight.
A heart of fire, fierce and bold,
In embered warmth, the tales unfold.

Through shadows deep, they dance and sway,
Beneath the stars, they find their way.
The past's embrace, a tender hand,
In every spark, a promise stands.

Oh, gentle cradle, hold them tight,
In vibrant hues of soft moonlight.
A phoenix born from dreams once lost,
Through every trial, love is the cost.

With wings of gold, they soar anew,
In realms of wonder, skies of blue.
Each heartbeat sings, a timeless rhyme,
In ashes cradle, transcending time.

Guardian of Celestial Stories

Upon the edge of night's embrace,
The guardian stands with a watchful grace.
With eyes like stars, they keep the watch,
Of cosmic tales, they do not botch.

From realms unseen, the echoes call,
Of whispered myths and ancients' thrall.
In moonlit beams, their stories weave,
The threads of fate that none perceive.

With every breath, a secret shared,
In cosmic dance, they show they cared.
For every heart that seeks to know,
The guardian guides, the starlight's glow.

In celestial realms where shadows blend,
With open arms, they seek to mend.
The stories linger, rich and vast,
In parchment skies, the die is cast.

The Wisdom Woven in Fire

In flickering flames, knowledge burns bright,
Each spark a whisper, a guiding light.
With tales of ages, both old and new,
In the heart of the blaze, the wise pursue.

Through trials faced and battles won,
From ashes cold, new legends spun.
A tapestry rich in hues of gold,
Each thread a lesson, a truth retold.

In fire's embrace, the spirits soar,
For every ending is just a door.
With every flame that dances free,
Wisdom emerges, like whispered glee.

Through shadows long, and winds that howl,
The fire speaks in a fervent growl.
In its glow, the heart finds peace,
In wisdom's warmth, all fears release.

Echoing Halls of Fiery Feats

In echoing halls where legends tread,
The whispers of heroes dance like thread.
With courage bold, their stories roam,
In fiery feats, they find their home.

Each step resounds with tales of yore,
Of victories claimed and challenges more.
In shadowed corners, the past awakes,
With every heartbeat, the earth quakes.

The flickered light reveals their names,
In shimmering sparks, they play their games.
Through trials fiery, they rise, they soar,
In echoing halls, forevermore.

For every heart that seeks to shine,
These echoing feats, a sacred sign.
In unity forged by fires' song,
In the halls of glory, we all belong.

Solar Reflections of a Myth

In the dawn's embrace, shadows dance,
Whispers of legends, a fleeting glance.
Golden rays kiss the earth anew,
Stories of old in bright hues imbued.

Mountains echo with secrets untold,
In the sun's warm glow, their courage unfolds.
Each beam carries lore from ages past,
Illuminating paths, an eternal cast.

Rivers sparkled, with dreams intertwined,
Reflecting the battles that history defined.
A light-woven tapestry of fate,
In every shimmer, the sun celebrates.

The winds carry murmurs of wisdom's flight,
A journey of souls in the shimmering light.
Through valleys and hills, their stories resound,
In this solar ballet, magic is found.

So rise with the sun, embrace the grand tale,
Of shadows and glories where ancients prevail.
For myth is alive in the warmth that we feel,
In solar reflections, our dreams become real.

Flame-Spun Whispers of Yore

Beneath the twilight, embers glow bright,
Carrying echoes of lost ancient light.
Flames twist and curl, like stories retold,
In their flickering dance, our futures unfold.

The night is alive with the lore of the past,
From shadowed corners, the memories cast.
Each spark a whisper from spirits so bold,
Bringing forth magic as secrets unfold.

Gathered around, with hearts full of dreams,
We listen intently, or so it seems.
The fire now crackles, a voice from the night,
Telling of heroes and their gallant fight.

With every crack, a tale takes its flight,
Of love and of loss in the flickering light.
Weaving together the threads of our fate,
In flame-spun whispers, we patiently wait.

So come, share your story, let the embers ignite,
In the warmth of the fire, find courage, take flight.
For time's but an illusion, a silken thread spun,
In the flame's gentle glow, we are all but one.

Vision of Phoenix Beneath Ancient Wings

In the depths of dusk, a shadow looms,
Wings of the ancients, through twilight blooms.
A phoenix ascends, from ashes reborn,
In its fiery flight, new hope is adorned.

Glistening feathers reflect stars above,
Echoes of courage, resilience, and love.
Soaring through dreams, with grace in the skies,
Awakening wonders, where destiny lies.

Each beat of its wings, a promise to keep,
In the night's embrace, where the lost dreams sleep.
Guided by stardust, it dances on air,
A vision of freedom, we long to declare.

In the heart of the storm, it thrives and it sings,
Born from the ashes, what magic it brings!
Through trials and flames, forever it flies,
A testament bright to our own lofty skies.

So watch for the phoenix, as night turns to day,
In its radiant glow, let our worries decay.
For beneath ancient wings, we find our own flight,
In the vision of hope, we embrace the light.

The Timeworn Guardian's Charge

Beneath the shadows, an ancient watch lies,
Guarding the realms where the forgotten sighs.
With eyes like the stars, and a heart of the past,
Standing in silence, an oath ever cast.

Each whispering breeze, a tale of its own,
Of battles once fought, of seeds that were sown.
In the tapestry woven with threads of delight,
Echoes the promise to safeguard the night.

Through ages long gone, it bears every mark,
Protecting the light against shadows so stark.
With wisdom as armor, a shield built of grace,
The guardian stands firm, a sentinel's place.

As time speeds on, with its relentless flow,
The stories evolve, and the seasons bestow.
Yet steadfast and true, the guardian remains,
In the heart of the woods, in the soft falling rains.

So heed the old tales of the timeworn embrace,
In the guardian's charge, find your own sacred space.
For through every challenge, every struggle we face,
We are all protected in this timeless place.

The Echo of Forgotten Flames

In shadows deep where whispers dwell,
The ancient fires weave their spell.
Memories dance in flickering light,
Rekindling dreams that fade from sight.

With every spark, a story stirs,
Of fallen leaves and silent murmurs.
Once bright embers now softly sigh,
As forgotten flames begin to fly.

The past ignites in hues of gold,
While secrets of the night unfold.
A calming warmth, an echo found,
In the stillness, history sounds.

Through corridors of time, they glide,
Awakening hearts where hope resides.
In the heart's chamber, softly pressed,
The flames remember; they never rest.

So listen close, for they impart,
The wisdom held within the heart.
As echoes fade into the night,
The forgotten flames ignite their light.

Flames Remember the First Song

When twilight drapes the world in peace,
The flames remember, never cease.
Their ancient tongues in silence weave,
The melodies from which we cleave.

A lullaby that spans the years,
Through laughter sweet and shattered fears.
In flickers bright, the notes resound,
A harmony no bounds have found.

Once sung beneath the starlit skies,
Where dreams took flight and spirits rise.
The first song hums in the ember glow,
A call to hearts that long to know.

From kindling sparks, the chorus grows,
In fiery arcs, its magic flows.
Each note a whisper, old yet new,
As flames remember what's pure and true.

And so, they burn, a steady guide,
The first song lingers, side by side.
In every heart, a silent throng,
Together, we sing the timeless song.

Watchful Eyes Over the Fiery Rebirth

In twilight's glow, when shadows blend,
The watchful eyes of fire ascend.
They guard the dreams that flicker bright,
In the dance of day, into the night.

With every spark, a whisper shared,
A promise made, a heart laid bare.
These flames, a symbol of rebirth,
With ancient lore, they warm the earth.

In every flicker, wisdom gleaned,
A testament to what has been.
Through trials faced, they stand so true,
Painting the sky in vibrant hue.

The watchful eyes, they never stray,
O'er sleep and slumber, they will stay.
As fiery tales take flight anew,
Their loving glow will guide us through.

So let us bask in this embrace,
The fiery warmth, a sacred space.
For in the light, we find our way,
Watchful eyes will never sway.

The Scribe of Flame and Shadow

In corners where the shadows play,
A scribe records the night and day.
With quill and flame, the story's spun,
Each flicker holds the weight of sun.

The ink is drawn from ashes old,
Of secrets kept and truths retold.
For every burn, a tale to share,
Of love and loss, of hope and despair.

The pages whisper in the dark,
As flames illuminate the spark.
Each word a dance, a fleeting ghost,
Of yearning hearts and what they've lost.

Through flame and shadow, truth will gleam,
Like stars reflected in a dream.
The scribe, a keeper of the flame,
In every shadow, speaks a name.

So gather close, let stories flow,
Of flame and shadow, ebb and glow.
In every line, a life reborn,
The scribe's promise will not be worn.

Tapestry of Ash and Embers

In the dusk where shadows play,
Threads of memories weave and fray.
Whispers linger, soft and low,
Through the ashes, embers glow.

Patterns dance, both bright and dim,
Echoes of a dream, so slim.
Fires fade but do not cease,
In their warmth, we find release.

Every spark a story told,
In the dark, the brave unfold.
A tapestry of fate entwined,
In the heart, the light we find.

Flickering flames reveal the truth,
Of lost laughter and fleeting youth.
In the silence, shadows loom,
From the ashes, life will bloom.

With every ember, a hope takes flight,
In the stillness, we unite.
Through the night, the stars will gleam,
In the ash, there lies a dream.

The Idol Beneath the Rising Fire

Beneath a sky of orange glow,
Lies an idol, lost to woe.
Twixt the flames, it waits in grace,
Yearning for a warm embrace.

The fire dances, shadows tease,
In the embers, ancient pleas.
Around the stone, the tales unfold,
Of whispered secrets, brave and bold.

Winds of change begin to howl,
As the flames in silence growl.
From ashes, heroes often rise,
To meet the dawn with fearless eyes.

In the glow, forgotten lore,
Awakens dreams from days of yore.
With burning passion burning bright,
The idol calls to those who fight.

Beneath the fire's watchful gaze,
New legends bloom, the past ablaze.
In the heat, the heart does soar,
Embracing all that came before.

Secrets of the Celestial Ember

In the night where silence reigns,
A single ember breaks the chains.
Spark of truth, so brightly found,
In the cosmos, dreams abound.

Whispers wrapped in starlit air,
Encounters brief yet eternally rare.
Through the darkness, visions glow,
Guiding hearts where few dare go.

Every flicker tells a tale,
Of brave souls who dared prevail.
In the shadows, light will bend,
Holding secrets without end.

Celestial fires guide the brave,
In the silence, the stars behave.
Veils of night begin to lift,
With every ember, a priceless gift.

Through the silence, echoes thrive,
In the ember, we come alive.
A constellation born anew,
In the vast, celestial blue.

Time's Phoenix in a Ring of Ash

In a ring where ashes lie,
Time's own phoenix learns to fly.
Caught between the dawn and dusk,
Fading shadows, stirring husk.

With each rebirth, a story grows,
In the echoes, the since exposure shows.
Cinders swirl, a dance of fate,
In the stillness, we await.

From the embers, life will spring,
As the phoenix begins to sing.
Rising high above the flames,
In the heart, it finds its names.

Round the circle, tales are spun,
Of victories lost and battles won.
In the heart where ashes rest,
Time's great phoenix finds its quest.

With every rise, destruction fades,
In the ashes, hope cascades.
A reminder of what has been,
In the cycle, we begin again.

Flameset Heritage

In the heart of the old, embers sigh,
Legends linger where whispers lie.
A tale of flames, fierce and bright,
Binding souls in the heart of night.

Blood runs warm with the spark of time,
Echoes of courage in rhythm and rhyme.
From ashes rise the strength we claim,
Carved in the stones, forever the same.

Cloaks of sunset, cloaks of pride,
Holding the past, forever our guide.
In every flicker, the hearth's good grace,
A lineage wrapped in the flames' embrace.

With every blaze, a promise made,
To honor the bonds that will not fade.
In hearth and home, we find our way,
A spark of the old in the light of day.

Together we stand 'neath the flickering light,
Guardians of dreams that take flight at night.
The stories we weave, in flames we trust,
A heritage bright, in fire, we must.

The Torchbearer's Embrace

In the shadows where silence sleeps,
A flicker of hope, a promise keeps.
For those who wander in search of light,
The torchbearer's call shines through the night.

Hands outstretched, a warmth to share,
Guiding the lost with tender care.
In the glow, a path unfolds,
A dance of tales yet to be told.

Embrace the flame that flickers near,
In the darkest moments, it draws us near.
With each soft breath, we find our place,
In the heart of the torch's warm embrace.

The weight of the world, a burden strong,
But the light we carry will guide us along.
In unity, we'll carry the flame,
For love is the torch that calls our name.

Together we rise, as night meets dawn,
In every heartbeat, a new hope drawn.
With the fire of kinship, we'll never part,
The torchbearer's light ignites every heart.

Ancestral Spirits in Fluency

Whispers of ages that weave through air,
Ancestral spirits with stories to share.
In every shadow, a voice will call,
Binding us close, one and all.

The language of hearts, in silence spoken,
Carried on winds, unbroken.
In dances of leaves, in rains that fall,
Echoes of wisdom, they guide us all.

With every tear, a lineage flows,
Through rivers of time, life's essence glows.
A tapestry rich with vibrant hue,
Woven by hands of those we knew.

In laughter and sorrow, their spirits dwell,
Stories of triumph, of trials we tell.
In every heartbeat, our roots entwine,
Their strength, our compass, their love, our sign.

So honor the past, let its voices sing,
The wisdom it brings, the hope it will bring.
In every moment of grace and beauty,
Ancestral spirits reveal their duty.

Winged Shadows of the Past

In the twilight sky, shadows take flight,
Winged whispers beckon the night.
Guardians of dreams that softly glide,
Carrying tales where hopes abide.

Through the shroud of dusk, their dances weave,
Echoes of stories that never leave.
In every rustle, a promise made,
In the hush of night, our fears allayed.

With feathers of silver, they trace the stars,
A symphony of hearts, our chosen avatars.
They guide us forth through darkness deep,
Awakening spirits from their sleep.

When the dawn breaks, their shadows remain,
Filling the air with joy and pain.
A bittersweet balm, they gently bring,
Hope through the songs of their silent wing.

Together we chase the shadows that roam,
With wings of the past, we find our home.
For in each flight, every gentle breeze,
Lies the strength of shadows, a soul's release.

The Cinders of Forgotten Embrace

In twilight's hush, where shadows play,
A lingering warmth, a soft decay.
Memories dance in embered light,
Two souls entwined, now out of sight.

The whispers call from ages past,
In silent halls where love was cast.
With every spark that softly fades,
A testament of bygone glades.

Yet in the dark, a glow remains,
The ache of loss, our longing gains.
A flicker here, a sighing breeze,
A heart that beats with fading ease.

Cinders glow under starlit skies,
Soft tendrils rise, a sweet reprise.
Though time may dim the fieriest flame,
The warmth within shall still reclaim.

In every shadow, every spark,
Lies the embrace, though cold and dark.
For love, forgotten, does not cease,
In every heart, it finds release.

The Ever-Present Protector

Beneath the stars, a watchful gaze,
In quiet strength, through fog and haze.
When darkness falls, and fears awake,
A gentle hand, no heart shall break.

The winds may howl, the storms may rage,
But in your soul, I turn the page.
With whispered vows and steadfast light,
I stand beside you through the night.

When shadows stretch, and tremors shake,
With every breath, my promise wakes.
Fear not the trials that come your way,
For I shall guard both night and day.

An anchor firm, in time's great sea,
I am the bond that sets you free.
Through every path, I'll guide your stride,
A constant force, always beside.

With gentle words, I'll soothe your mind,
In the chaos, peace you'll find.
Through life's tempestuous stormy flight,
I'll be your ever-present light.

Glorious Echoes from the Spark

In every fire, a story told,
Of dreams ignited, and hearts of gold.
With every flicker, a new refrain,
The dance of hope, through joy and pain.

Echoes linger, in the starlit air,
Resounding joy, love's sweet affair.
From ashes rise, a vibrant tale,
Of spirits bold that will prevail.

Each glowing ember, a promise made,
In shadows deep, where memories wade.
A chorus sung with fervent mirth,
The celebration of our worth.

Through every spark, a light shall beam,
Illuminating every dream.
Life's profound, intricate art,
With glorious echoes that never part.

So gather 'round, beneath the moon,
And let our hearts share this sweet tune.
For as long as fires gently spark,
We'll hear the echoes in the dark.

Flames That Brush the Soul

A flicker soft, in twilight's wane,
A warmth that soothes the hidden pain.
With every blaze, a heart's desire,
The tender glow of purest fire.

When evening falls, and dreams take flight,
The flames will brush, igniting night.
A dance of passions, fierce and bright,
As shadows weave, in feathered light.

With every crackle, hope is found,
In joyful whispers, love's sweet sound.
From ashes rise, emotions swirl,
In the tender sway of a daring world.

The embers sing of all we seek,
In moments brave, when hearts grow weak.
Let love's fierce warmth, a guiding toll,
Be flames that brush and mend the soul.

So gather close, embrace the fire,
Feed the blaze of your heart's desire.
For in this light, we shall create,
A world of dreams, where love awaits.

A Watcher in the Ashen Dawn

In the soft glow of morning's breath,
A figure stands by the edge of time.
With eyes like embers, watching death,
In silence, he waits, a watcher sublime.

The skies paint tales in strokes of grey,
Promises whispered in the fading light.
Yet hope stirs softly, a gentle sway,
Awakening dreams that take to flight.

Mist clings to branches like tender hands,
Shadows dance where secrets weave.
In this realm where nothing stands,
A heart once lost now learns to believe.

The ashen dawn unveils its lore,
Each flicker a story, told in sighs.
The silence echoes, forevermore,
As courage ignites beneath the skies.

With every moment, the watcher knows,
Each fleeting spark a chance to mend.
In the ashen dawn where wonder grows,
A new beginning, a tale without end.

Shadows Cast by Ancient Wings

Beneath the canopy of twilight's grace,
Ancient wings unfurl with might.
In whispers soft, they leave no trace,
Shrouded in mysteries, lost to sight.

Through forest deep and wild they soar,
Casting shadows on the earth below.
Legends breathed in the night's implore,
As echoes of ages begin to flow.

With every flap, a tremor wakes,
A gentle stirring in slumbering trees.
The world holds its breath, the stillness breaks,
As shadows linger on the evening breeze.

From heights unseen, they guard the land,
Ancestors' wishes, woven and true.
In the dark, they extend their hand,
Guiding lost souls to paths anew.

With every dusk, the stories blend,
Shadows cast where the heart ignites.
In the flight of creatures who dare to descend,
Lies the strength to conquer the nights.

The Grasp of Time and Fire

In the flicker of flame, a moment spins,
Time entwined with a fiery embrace.
Dance of the ages where truth begins,
A tapestry woven in chaotic grace.

Embers whisper tales of the past,
They crackle with laughter, sorrow, and dreams.
Through the veil of years, the shadows cast,
Reveal the glow of forgotten gleams.

In twilight's grip, the echoes laugh,
A symphony played by the hands of fate.
Each heartbeat a note, a cherished half,
In the rhythm of life, we navigate.

Fire swirls gently, a magic untold,
With every flicker, a wish takes flight.
As time unravels its threads of gold,
We grasp at starlight, embracing the night.

Beyond horizons where shadows retreat,
The grasp of time in its fiery guise,
In dreams eternal where moments meet,
We find our truth in the silent skies.

Whispers from the Celestial Staff

Beyond the clouds where stardust sings,
A staff of light cuts through the dark.
It cradles the cosmos, holds ancient springs,
As whispers echo through night's remark.

In the tender space between breath and thought,
Ancient voices beckon with grace.
Every flickering spark reveals what's sought,
A map to the heart, a navigated place.

With every shimmer, a calling clear,
The universe weaves its intricate plot.
In the silence of wonder, we draw near,
To secrets that time has nearly forgot.

Through the veil of stars, the visions soar,
Each flick of the wrist, a tale to unveil.
The celestial staff opens heaven's door,
Guiding lost dreams where wishes sail.

In the glow of twilight, the world aligns,
A harmony crafted in celestial art.
With whispers from beyond, the cosmos shines,
Each echo a promise, a brand new start.

The Age-Old Sentinel's Embrace

In woods where whispers linger long,
An ancient tree stands proud and strong.
Its roots entwined with stories lost,
A guardian standing, no matter the cost.

Beneath its branches, dreams take flight,
In shadowed corners, hearts ignite.
The sentinel watches, silent and wise,
Embracing the secrets held within skies.

A rustle of leaves tells tales of old,
Of love, of courage, forever bold.
Each bough a memory, a time gone by,
An endless bond 'neath the vast, blue sky.

Its bark is worn, the years unfold,
Yet still it stands, through heat and cold.
Its sturdy limbs, a haven sought,
In its embrace, all battles are fought.

So here we gather, in its shade,
To share our dreams, our fears conveyed.
With cedar scent and twilight's grace,
We find our peace in the sentinel's embrace.

Flames Danced by Ageless Eyes

In a hearth where shadows twine,
A flicker glows, a spark divine.
The flames, they dance, alive, aware,
In silence, they weave the warmth of air.

Old eyes behold the fire's plight,
Reflecting embers in soft twilight.
Stories whispered in each flicker,
A timeless bond, the moments thicker.

Each blaze a heartbeat, wild and free,
Ancient tales in flickering glee.
Cocooned by warmth, we cease to roam,
In flames, we find our way back home.

Through years and ages, they have burned,
By ageless eyes, the wisdom learned.
A circle formed by night's embrace,
Where dreams ignite, and shadows trace.

So gather 'round, and feel the glow,
Of passions kindled, hearts that know.
In this sacred light, we shall rejoice,
With flames that dance and call our voice.

Secrets Beneath the Rustling Feathers

In twilight's hush, where secrets nest,
Beneath the wings of a stoic guest.
Feathers whisper tales of old,
Of journeys taken, and legends told.

An owl takes flight, through velvet skies,
Echoes of wisdom in its wise eyes.
It knows the paths where starlight weaves,
And wraps our dreams in silver leaves.

Beneath each plume, a mystery sleeps,
In shadows deep where silence keeps.
A feather falls, a gentle sigh,
Carrying whispers, both low and high.

Through haunted woods, its spirit glides,
With every flutter, the past abides.
And in the stillness, we hear the call,
Of ancient stories that bind us all.

So tread lightly where secrets lay,
In rustling feathers, they gently sway.
Embrace the night, let wonders flow,
For in the darkness, our spirits grow.

A Legacy Intertwined with Ember

In an ember's glow, a tale begins,
Of hearts entwined and timeless sins.
Ashes whisper of the past we tread,
While the future dances, bright, ahead.

A legacy forged in fire's embrace,
Where laughter lingers, time can't erase.
Each flicker sparks a memory dear,
Of those we've loved and held so near.

As night descends, the embers speak,
Of strength and courage in moments weak.
They weave our stories, both joyous and grave,
In every glow, a soul to save.

The flames now dim, yet still they shine,
A bond unbroken, forever divine.
With every spark, our hearts ignite,
A legacy wrapped in warmth and light.

So let us gather, hand in hand,
In the warmth of fires where memories stand.
For through the ember, love will spark,
An everlasting flame in the dark.

Beneath the Smoldering Sky

Beneath the sky, a smoldering hue,
Whispers of ashes, carried anew.
The echoes of battles, long since past,
Dance on the winds, in shadows cast.

With every ember, a story unfolds,
Of heroes and legends, of courage bold.
In twilight's embrace, the night sings low,
While stars bear witness to the ebb and flow.

Through the veil of darkness, a flicker of light,
Guides wandering souls through the endless night.
A tapestry woven with threads of fate,
Unraveling moments that lie in wait.

The moon weeps silver, her tears like dew,
Over dreams forgotten, and hopes untrue.
Yet in the silence, a promise remains,
Of love unbroken, through joy and pains.

As dawn approaches, the shadows retreat,
Revealing the path where lost hearts meet.
Beneath the smoldering sky, we find grace,
In the glow of tomorrow, we embrace.

Herald of the Celestial Fire

In the heart of night, the fire ignites,
A herald of truths, a beacon of sights.
With flames that shimmer, like stars in flight,
It whispers of hope, in shadows of light.

The winds carry tales through the cosmic sea,
Of destinies woven, of you and me.
Each flicker a promise, each blaze a sign,
Calling us forth, to realms divine.

From embers of chaos, new worlds arise,
Crafted by dreams under open skies.
The celestial fire ignites our souls,
A journey of magic, where passion unfolds.

With every heartbeat, the universe sings,
Of divine connections and wondrous things.
A tapestry woven with love and desire,
We dance on the winds, as heralds of fire.

So fear not the shadows that cloud your way,
For light shall emerge, come what may.
In the arms of the cosmos, forever we soar,
Heralds of fire, forevermore.

Resurgence Beneath Gilded Feathers

Amidst the ruins where silence reigns,
Life stirs anew, despite all the pains.
Beneath gilded feathers, the heart shall bloom,
Emerging from darkness, dispelling the gloom.

With whispers of hope, the stories revive,
In the cradle of dreams, we learn to thrive.
Each feather a token of love's sweet refrain,
Carried by spirits that dance in the rain.

The tapestry woven, with threads of gold,
Of ancient desires and tales retold.
Through trials of fire, our spirits ascend,
Resurrected by love, as the shadows bend.

The sky will remember the songs of our past,
In echoes of laughter, eternally cast.
Amidst the ashes, our souls take flight,
Bound by the magic of endless light.

So rise from the ashes, let courage lead,
For beneath gilded feathers lies the seed.
A resurgence of strength, a boundless grace,
In the heart of the storm, we find our place.

Keeper of the Cindered Legacy

In the twilight hours, where shadows creep,
The keeper awakens from long restless sleep.
With cindered pages, the story unfolds,
Of ancient legends and truths untold.

Whispers of wisdom, carried on air,
Guide the wayfarers through valleys of despair.
The echoes of laughter, the sighs of the past,
In the heart of the keeper, forever they'll last.

With a flick of the wrist, the embers ignite,
Painting the darkness with hues of bright light.
For every heart yearning, a path shall appear,
Leading us onward, dispelling all fear.

Through the fires of trials, our spirits are forged,
In the flames of remembrance, courage engorged.
A legacy cindered, yet fiercely alive,
In the keeper's embrace, our dreams will survive.

So gather your stories, let them be known,
In the keeper's heart, no one is alone.
For from the cinders, new flames will arise,
A timeless connection, beneath starry skies.

The Warden of Rejuvenation

In the glade where whispers dwell,
A guardian stands, casting a spell.
With every leaf and every sigh,
Nature's promise to never die.

The brook flows soft, a gentle guide,
Where secrets of old in waters hide.
Restoration, like morning's light,
Shows us all that wrong can right.

Beneath the boughs of ancient trees,
The air is rich with sweet release.
Hope rekindled with each new dawn,
In this haven, fears are gone.

A mosaic of life, woven tight,
With shadows dancing in the night.
Here, every creature finds its place,
In the embrace of time's warm grace.

Fear not the trials that life will send,
For the warden's care shall never end.
Through storms and trials, take your stand,
With rejuvenation close at hand.

The Light That Endures

In twilight's hush, a beacon glows,
A flicker bright where hope still flows.
Through tangled paths and darkest fears,
This light remains, through all the years.

When shadows creep and spirits tire,
It whispers kindness, sends desire.
With every spark, it fans the flame,
Binding hearts, igniting names.

In moments lost, and dreams confined,
A glow persists through heart and mind.
It beckons souls to rise and soar,
To find their strength and seek for more.

Though tempests rage and doubts collide,
This constant warmth shall be our guide.
Forever shining through it all,
The light that endures will never fall.

Embrace the glimmer, trust the glow,
For every journey starts to grow.
With courage found in passion's fire,
We walk the path that leads us higher.

Into the Past's Glowing Embrace

Upon the bridge of memories made,
With every step, the past won't fade.
The echoes linger, soft and sweet,
In corners where our dreams repeat.

Through time's embrace, the stories flow,
Of laughter bright and tears that glow.
Each chapter rich with lessons learned,
In heart's own hearth, the candles burned.

We wander back through ages known,
In fleeting glimpses, truth is sown.
With open arms, history waits,
To teach us all of life's great fates.

Beneath the stars, where secrets lie,
We anchor hopes and let them fly.
Connected threads of joy and pain,
In this embrace, we find our gain.

A tapestry of moments bright,
Guides us through the depth of night.
So, step with grace, with heart laid bare,
Into the past's eternal care.

Timeless Flames and Forged Fables

When ember's pulse ignites the dark,
And ancient tales begin to spark.
The flames are stories, fierce and bold,
Of heroes lost and legends told.

Through whispered winds and shadows cast,
Each flicker carries echoes vast.
Forged in trials, hope ignites,
As dreams are shaped with lovers' rights.

The hearth of life holds warmth and grace,
In timeless flames, we find our place.
With every flick, our hearts align,
As fables dance through space and time.

When darkness looms, let courage swell,
For tales of strength in hearts will dwell.
Together, we'll stand hand in hand,
For forged fables form a steadfast band.

So gather 'round, let stories brew,
In kindled light, we'll start anew.
With every word, the night shall lilt,
In timeless flames, our hope is built.

The Ember's Eternal Vigil

In shadows deep, the ember glows,
A watchful eye where no one goes.
Through whispered winds and twilight's sigh,
It guards the flame as time drifts by.

With flickering dance, it weaves the night,
A sentinel of fading light.
Against the dark, it stands alone,
A beacon bright for hearts of stone.

As dreams take flight on dusky wings,
The ember hums, and softly sings.
With every spark, a story told,
Of courage found in embers bold.

So heed the warmth that softly speaks,
In quiet moments, truth it seeks.
For in the glow of what remains,
Eternal life through fiery veins.

A vigil kept, the echoes ring,
In every heart, the ember's sting.
With gentle flames that never tire,
It holds the world, a living fire.

Custodian of the Reborn Light

Upon the hill where shadows play,
The custodian waits for break of day.
In hands of fate, he cradles dreams,
To stitch the night with golden seams.

With ancient whispers, time unfolds,
The reborn light, a tale retold.
From ashes borne, new hopes arise,
A promise held beneath the skies.

Through veils of darkness, paths entwine,
He guards the fate of worlds divine.
With every dawn that paints the sky,
He breathes the truth, and wonders sigh.

In moonlit realms, his spirit glows,
A quiet strength, as knowledge flows.
Through trials faced, the heart will learn,
That from the dark, the light will burn.

For every sorrow, joy will bloom,
In shadows cast, dispelling gloom.
The custodian stands by the flame,
A keeper true of nature's name.

The Keeper of Scorched Dreams

In memories steeped in ash and fire,
The keeper wanders, lost in desire.
With haunted eyes, he tends the past,
In scorched terrain where shadows cast.

He gathers whispers of long-lost cries,
Entwined with stars in shattered skies.
Each broken dream, a tale forlorn,
He mends with care, though hearts are worn.

Through twisted paths of sorrow's grace,
He finds a flicker, a fleeting trace.
In darkest depths, where spirits wail,
He conjures light from every trail.

With every breath, remembrance swells,
The keeper knows what silence tells.
Through fire's dance, redemption gleams,
To forge anew from scorched dreams.

From every tear, a strength will rise,
In smoldered hope beneath the skies.
For in the ashes, futures dwell,
The keeper waits, a silent bell.

The Glimmering Sentinel of Time

In twilight's glow, a figure stands,
The sentinel with silvered hands.
He weaves a tapestry of fate,
In shimmering threads, both small and great.

With visions vast, he charts the flow,
Of every heartbeat, ebbs, and throes.
Through ages past, his watchful gaze,
Lifts every soul from time's dark maze.

With whispered truths, he crafts the night,
In starlit dreams that burn so bright.
For every moment, fleeting grace,
He holds them dear in time's embrace.

With glimmering eyes, he knows the score,
Of lives entwined and tales of yore.
Through every dawn, a promise made,
The sentinel guards the light that swayed.

So trust in paths the stars align,
In secret steps, through realms divine.
For time will turn, and shadows fade,
The glimmering sentinel's serenade.

Entrusted with the Spirit of Fire

In shadows dark where whispers play,
The flame ignites the night to day.
With every spark, a tale unfurls,
Of bravery found in hidden worlds.

The heartbeats dance with embers bright,
Guiding lost souls through the night.
Entrusted hands, the torch we bear,
To light the path in fields of air.

Through trials fierce and misty dreams,
The spirit burns, or so it seems.
With courage forged in furnace fire,
Our spirits soar, ever higher.

Bound to the flame, our souls entwined,
In every flicker, fate aligned.
With whispered vows, we rise and tread,
Where ancient echoes softly spread.

As guardians of the sacred light,
We carry forth the hope so bright.
In hearts aflame, we find our voice,
Together we stand, united in choice.

Heartbeats Beneath a Fiery Sky

Underneath the glowing hues,
Where twilight meets the dusk's fond views.
Heartbeats echo in the air,
A symphony without a care.

Beneath the stars, the embers glow,
Whispers of secrets only night can know.
In passion's breath, the dreams ignite,
Guiding our souls through the endless night.

The world awakens with each sigh,
As fiery clouds drift slowly by.
In that moment, time suspends,
As destiny draws nearer, friends.

The warmth of hearts, a radiant beam,
Carving paths like a woven dream.
Beneath the fiery, scried-up sky,
We find our courage, we learn to fly.

Together we stand, hand in hand,
In the embrace of this golden land.
As heartbeats pulse and stars align,
In every challenge, we shall shine.

Threnody for a Rising Soul

In silence deep, the echoes fall,
A threnody for one and all.
With wings unfurled, a spirit free,
Awakens the dawn's melody.

We sing for those who've forged the way,
Through trials dark, in night's dismay.
With tender grace, they rise again,
Guided by love, through joy and pain.

A whispered note, a crimson cry,
As stars embrace the velvet sky.
Each tear they shed, a diamond bright,
Illuminating paths with light.

Within the heart, their stories throng,
A dance of shadows, fierce and strong.
For every soul that's dared to soar,
We find their song forevermore.

Let memories weave a golden thread,
Through skies once blue, where hope had fled.
Each note they played, a cherished role,
Resounding still, their rising soul.

When Flames Yield to Silent Guardians

When flames yield to the still of night,
Silent guardians cloak the light.
In veils of dusk, they gently tread,
With whispers soft, where dreams are fed.

In shadows deep, they softly loom,
A watchful presence, guarding gloom.
With every crackle, their wisdom shares,
The strength in silence, beauty cares.

In twilight's arms, their spirits dance,
A glimmer found in fate's sweet chance.
When chaos reigns in shadows cold,
They weave a tale of hearts so bold.

As flames retreat, their glow remains,
In echoes sweet, the heart sustains.
Through trials steep and roads untold,
The silent guides bring warmth from cold.

In darkest hours, they stand so near,
Their steadfast hearts dispel all fear.
When flames yield to the night's embrace,
The guardians shine in humbleness and grace.

The Ageless Dance of Renewal

In twilight's glow, the shadows sway,
The whispers of the night begin to play.
Beneath the stars, the world takes flight,
In endless rhythms, we find our light.

The seasons turn, with gentle grace,
Nature's pulse in a sacred space.
Petals fall, yet roots remain,
From earth to sky, a sweet refrain.

With every dawn, a chance to heal,
In tender moments, we feel what's real.
The heart's brave song, both soft and strong,
A timeless dance where we belong.

The cycle spins, in perfect time,
We write our tales in verse and rhyme.
In every ending, a brand new start,
Renewed by love, we play our part.

So let us dance through night and day,
In harmony, we'll find our way.
With open arms, the world we greet,
In the ageless dance, our spirits meet.

Celestial Guardian's Burning Echo

When stars align in velvet skies,
A guardian whispers, soft and wise.
With wings of light, they soar above,
Their burning echo sings of love.

In shadows deep, when hope feels thin,
They guide our hearts, igniting within.
With every breath, the fire glows,
An ancient warmth that brightly shows.

From cosmic realms, their gaze is known,
In silent battles, seeds are sown.
A flicker fierce in darkest night,
They stand as shields, our inner light.

Through trials faced, their strength, our shield,
A promise kept, a fate revealed.
In every tear, in every smile,
Their echo lingers, fierce and wild.

So lift your eyes to heavens high,
Feel their presence, hear their cry.
For in the dance of time and space,
The celestial guardian finds their place.

Embrace of the Reborn Spirit

In gentle winds, the spirit stirs,
A vibrant echo, life confers.
With tender hands, the past undone,
In rebirth's glow, a new day won.

From ashes cold, the phoenix soars,
Through trials shaped, we find our cores.
The heart ignites, a flame anew,
In sacred cycles, we're born true.

With open hearts, we shed our chains,
Through joy and sorrow, love remains.
In every heartbeat, truth unfolds,
A timeless story, beautifully told.

Embrace the dawn with all your might,
In every shadow, find your light.
For in the depths, the spirit rises,
And love's embrace, the soul surprises.

In sacred dance, we find our way,
Like flowers bloom from coldest clay.
Reborn, we shine, a tapestry,
In life's embrace, we're truly free.

Nurtured by Timeless Flames

Beneath the stars, in cozy night,
Timeless flames keep spirits bright.
With every flicker, stories weave,
In sacred warmth, we dare believe.

Through crackling wood, the past exhales,
In every breath, the heart unveils.
The glow of hope in joy and pain,
A bond eternal, we sustain.

Nurtured deep by ember's glow,
In whispered tales, our spirits grow.
Each flickering spark, a memory,
Of what was lost, and yet can be.

The dance of flames in rhythmic play,
Unfolds the dreams of yesterday.
From gentle sparks to blazing fire,
Together, hearts can rise much higher.

So gather near, let shadows blend,
For in this warmth, our hearts transcend.
Nurtured by flames, we stand as one,
In the glow of love, our journey's begun.

Informing the Spirit of Rebirth

In shadows deep where whispers dwell,
A spark ignites, an unseen spell.
From ashes rise, a chance to mend,
New life awaits, old wounds to end.

Each tear that falls, a lesson learned,
Through bitter nights, the heart has burned.
Yet dawn will come, a brighter day,
With every breath, the past to sway.

A song of hope, in softest breeze,
Awakens dreams that seek to please.
So let the spirit softly soar,
Embracing all, forevermore.

With tender hands, the fate we weave,
In cycles spun, we learn to believe.
For every end births new delight,
In every shadow, emerges light.

The Keeper of Fiery Heirlooms

In twilight's glow, the secrets burn,
A keeper waits, for tales to turn.
With ember's grace, the past ignites,
In hearts of those who seek the sights.

Of heirlooms forged in summer's blaze,
Each flicker holds our ancient gaze.
For through the flames, the wisdom flows,
A legacy that always grows.

From molten gold to silver bright,
The keeper guards the flickering light.
With every spark, a memory sings,
A dance of truth on fiery wings.

In vaults of time where legends dwell,
The keeper knows each fiery spell.
In stories told by crackling fire,
Our dreams arise, our hearts aspire.

From Ashes to Insight

From ashes cold, the phoenix wakes,
With wings spread wide, the silence breaks.
In midst of chaos, clarity shines,
Emerging truth in twisted lines.

The fire within, a guiding flame,
In moments lost, we're never tame.
For through the trials, the heart expands,
In seeking life with open hands.

With every loss comes greater gain,
A lesson writ in joy and pain.
So rise anew, defy the night,
Transform the dark into pure light.

With eyes set forth, we journey far,
From ashes strewn, we'll find our star.
For in the depths, our spirit learns,
In every soul, a phoenix burns.

Twilight's Emissary and the Phoenix's Heart

A messenger of twilight's glow,
With feathered grace, the breezes blow.
In realms where dreams and dusk unfold,
The phoenix sings of tales retold.

With every beat, the heart ignites,
In whispered words, the spirit lights.
Embracing all, both dark and bright,
For every ending, a new flight.

The emissary with eyes of fire,
Guides weary souls to their desire.
In twilight's hush, where shadows part,
Awakens hope in the phoenix's heart.

As starlit skies weave night's embrace,
The ember glows, revealing grace.
With wings unfurled, we journey on,
Through twilight's warmth, a brand new dawn.

When Time Dances with Fire

In twilight's grasp, the embers sway,
Flickering tales of yesterday.
A whisper soft, a flame's embrace,
Where shadows lend their fleeting grace.

The hourglass sings of fading light,
In dance with fire, they take flight.
Each crackling spark, a memory spun,
In the heart's hearth, all battles won.

As time unfolds, the yarns entwine,
The past ignites in colors fine.
In every glow, a path revealed,
To dreams of old, our spirits healed.

Eagerly we chase the glow,
Through fleeting moments, swift and slow.
In the warmth of flames, we learn to fight,
Embraced by the shadows that fill the night.

So let us dance, both wild and free,
With fire and time, eternally.
For every beat, a story told,
In glowing arcs, in hues of gold.

Hold Fast the Refulgent Wisdom

In whispers old, the secrets lie,
Beneath the weight of an ancient sky.
Through tomes of lore, our minds do roam,
Finding light where shadows comb.

Hold fast the truths, the guiding light,
With wisdom's fire, we ignite the night.
Each lesson learned, a treasure spent,
In quests of heart, our souls' intent.

As echoes fade, the words remain,
In every joy, in every pain.
They weave a fabric, rich and bold,
A tapestry of stories told.

With open arms, we greet the dawn,
Embracing wisdom, ever drawn.
To know is to grow, to seek, to find,
In the quiet spaces, hearts aligned.

Now cherish every whispered thought,
For in their grasp, the truth is caught.
Hold fast the refulgent wisdom's flame,
The world awakens, never the same.

Ember Shadows Beneath Crumbling Stars

The night descends, with secrets profound,
In ember shadows, dreams are found.
Beneath the stars that flicker and fall,
Whispers echo in the silence's thrall.

Crumbling wishes, they fade away,
Yet hope ignites in a flickering sway.
The universe cradles all that remains,
In quiet corners, where stillness reigns.

Time's gentle hand molds tales anew,
As shadows dance in the twilight's hue.
With every breath, a wish is sewn,
In the fabric of night, we are never alone.

Fingers trace paths of forgotten dreams,
In the glow of embers, where magic gleams.
Lost in the cosmos, we silently plead,
For stars to listen, to nurture our need.

Ember shadows, don't let me sway,
From the crumbling stars that light my way.
In the vast expanse, let dreams take flight,
For in their glow, we find our light.

A Whiff of Ancient Ash

The air is thick with stories untold,
A whiff of ash, a memory bold.
In fleeting smoke, the echoes glide,
Of battles fought, of nations died.

Cinders whisper of times long past,
In every breath, those moments cast.
From the remnants, wisdom does rise,
In flickers, we glimpse the skies.

The warmth of flame, the weight of time,
In every gust, the roots of rhyme.
The ancient ash, a shroud of grace,
Binding our hearts to a timeless space.

With every flicker, a tale ignites,
Of love and loss, of endless nights.
In the dance of smoke, we face the truth,
An alchemy rich with age and youth.

So let us breathe in the fragrant past,
From ashes rise, unyielding and vast.
For in the whiff, our spirits soar,
Beyond the fire, forevermore.

www.ingramcontent.com/pod-product-compliance
Ingram Content Group UK Ltd.
Pitfield, Milton Keynes, MK11 3LW, UK
UKHW021416220125
4239UKWH00007B/112